THE LITTLE BOOK
OF INFLUENCE

THE LITTLE BOOK OF INFLUENCE

Helping Visionaries to Become New Earth Influencers

Inarra Aryane Griffyn, with Mark Futterman

Waterside Productions

Copyright © 2021 by Inarra Aryane Griffyn

All rights reserved. This book or any portion thereof may not be reproduced or used in any manner whatsoever without the express written permission of the publisher except for the use of brief quotations in articles and book reviews.

Printed in the United States of America

First Printing, 2021

ISBN-13: 978-1-951805-37-1 print edition
ISBN-13: 978-1-951805-38-8 ebook edition

Waterside Productions
2055 Oxford Ave
Cardiff, CA 92007
www.waterside.com

Dedicated to the activists, the environmentalists, the indigenous, the spiritual teachers, the disrupters ... and everyone who realizes things need to change but isn't yet sure what to do about it.

also to my father Tom Hutchinson who has spent his life working to bring environmental practice into being, globally. He who created roof gardens and roof meadows. He who champions organic practice and the humanitarian care of animals. I was always proud to be your daughter and proud of you as my father. This is you running though me.

A SPECIAL THANK YOU

During the Spring of 2019, I attended a Coaching Mastermind in San Diego. The main coach asked us to count from one to five sequentially through the seating arrangement of a large forum, and later when we remembered our number, I was sent to sit with the coaches who were sitting at table 5. I remember having a thought that as I hadn't ended up sitting with anyone I knew, there may be something important about to happen. This often happens in my life. I have a strong feeling of something conspiring.

At that table were Jenny Cornbleet and Mark Futterman who were helping us with our messaging. These two quiet souls, who offer their services wholeheartedly and with a humble attitude, struck a chord in me—something that I couldn't quite put my finger on. Jenny, the philosopher, asked questions that caused me to reflect deeply on my message, and Mark, the magician, then magically shifted the emphasis and tone of the message to shine more brightly than you can ever imagine possible. It was a short meeting.

A couple of months later I was driving in London and out of seemingly nowhere I got a strong message to write a book with them. I contacted them and told them it was a surprise myself to be choosing to write my next book *with* them, but would they consider it? I told them that at that time in my life I didn't want to be inward focused and have my head in a laptop. So, we created a new possibility that we would work throughout the year by Zoom (they were in many places as was I for these calls), and

I would verbally download my ideas and chapters and then Mark would shape the copy from the perspective of the audience.

The journey was wilder than I could ever have imagined. We became co-conspirators in the creation of The Little Book Of Influence. We laughed our heads off so many times. Often the sessions were hard to contain because we loved the subject matter so much, it inspired us personally to talk about our lives. They then came over to London and Glastonbury to attend one of my retreats. Something alchemically altered our little group in the sacred lands of the heart chakra of the world, Glastonbury. The relationship between the three of us deepened as did Mark and Jenny's understanding of and deep resonance with the work the work that I do.

What we created cannot be quantified. I have immense gratitude for my friends helping me pour this book out into the world. Thank you, Mark and Jenny, for stirring questions that brought this book to life. Thank you, Mark, for writing it with me. Thank you, Jenny, for your observations and thoughts that deepened the book and made it better. We were due to spend lots of time together journeying this summer, but instead Covid has caused us to stay put. Next year I feel this will be a time to meet again in the flesh and we can travel together to many realms and create together again. Friends indeed. Friends helping each other be better than if it was a solo journey. Much, much, gratitude.

TABLE OF CONTENTS

Preface xi
Introduction xv

Chapter 1 1
Chapter 2 7
Chapter 3 18
Chapter 4 23
Chapter 5 28
Chapter 6 38
Chapter 7 43
Chapter 8 48

PREFACE

It's The Summer Solstice 2020, and this year there's a powerful symbolic alignment. On the 21st of June, the full sun of the Solstice awakens with a new moon on the same day. I have been a student of symbols, a High Priestess of the ancient pathways of Britain and Ireland, and a branding expert for many years. Symbology speaks to my Soul. This is a birth of the New Earth.

The emerging Divine Feminine arrives with full potent expression. There is an invitation awaiting all of us. We are invited to meet our full expression of Divine Masculine and let out a howl.

Who are you?

What is your calling?

Your Tribe is listening.

If you take up this call at the emergence of New Earth, we will release a convergence of rivers of expression for humanity, the animals and Mother Earth. This is a reset. We walk now with eyes wide open.

It's not enough to notice the damage and move on. It's about solution based, eco-sustainable New Earth thought leaders connecting en-masse, using the best of digital systems to reunite desperate nomads. We call to each other to awaken and bring forth your answers.

We need *you* to step up now. No hiding, no "I'm not good enough." We simply don't have time.

Animals are going extinct year after year. Tribal leaders face the same fate; their ageless wisdom, that healed and taught the next generations sitting around the fire, is being lost.

In the days preceding the Pause (Corona Virus lockdown), I had instinctively tapped into the wisdom of a modern futurist Influencer, Roger James Hamilton. In his group of online entrepreneurs meeting as GeniusU—as Roger believes everyone has genius if they flow naturally toward the path of least resistance—I witnessed his authentic leadership.

Responding to the Covid 19 crisis, he delivered a futuristic vision of the crash of the US dollar and the greater turmoil of the collapse of America's economic system and how this will reverberate around the world. He spoke of Crisis Leadership and created a training which I myself took part in, becoming one of the Crisis Leadership Academy Faculty members. From this place, I have already pivoted and taken my business to the next level and my work is now the work of inspiration.

I hope this book inspires you to do something!

There are no accidents that this book, The Little Book of Influence, is about responding to the call of New Earth, as Roger calls it, Society 5.0. I had written about how influence has, at its root meaning, Fluv or flow like a river and how movements can emerge when influencers step up.

During the Corona Pandemic, we experienced the global uprising of the Black Lives Matter movement in response to the horrific murder of George Floyd by US police, which was caught on video and seen around the world. George Floyd's pleas of "I can't breathe" became a rallying cry and ignited a revolution, dare we say an *evolution*. I'd personally like to honor him here.

As the movement takes hold, and I am in conversation supporting Black and Indigenous communities to balance the vast backlog of white racist history, something much more than one cause has catalyzed into being.

The theme of suffocation is echoed in how Coronavirus attacks the lungs, and how the lungs of the planet are being decimated by loggers in the Amazon and elsewhere.

We humans need to breathe.

We are waking up.

A New Earth is being visioned into existence.

A healer friend of mine, an amazing inspirational Shamana, once said to me "every day, practice visioning the Earth you want to walk upon. Not the trauma. What we focus on, we magnify." So, it's time to magnify images of all people happy, expressed and free: of lions and cheetahs breeding and roaming: of artificial intelligence spreading all the ancient wisdom. For we are the many tribes of the rainbow, sitting around the fire of connection and healing.

We all have an absolute responsibility to vision New Earth in. Holding the space to rage and honoring those who need us to listen. In the listening comes the stillness and a new language of connection. It is my deepest desire to speak to your hearts and cause a stir so that you stand up and give us your magic.

We need everyone to speak the language of solution and to cause a shift of consciousness.

This is an invitation.

Hold out your hand and take mine and let's go!

INTRODUCTION

Humanity is at a choice point of epic proportions, and you, simply as someone walking on this earth right now, have a critical role to play.

So, if you are ready to do something positive… this time is for you. And so is this book.

The Little Book of Influence is about moving into the powerful work your heart yearns for you to do.

Each chapter is a reflection on some aspect of having influence. Along the way, you'll get questions to consider, visualizations to bring you clarity, stories of other influencers to give you inspiration, and lots of prodding to go out there and do what's calling to you.

We'll ask you to adopt certain ideas that you might not instantly resonate with. That's okay. We're only asking you to act "as if" they're true while you're here with us in these pages. Then, you can decide whether continuing to act that way helps you live and lead with more motivation, courage, and clarity.

Uncovering what you most want to influence and how you'll start doing it is the big goal of this little book.

So, let's get started!

CHAPTER 1

Influencers don't change the system... they create a new one!
"Influence" isn't about spouting your emotional reactions—you become an influencer by aligning with the evolution that wants to happen.

What exactly is an "influencer"?

Merriam-Webster gives two definitions:

- A person who inspires or guides the actions of others
- A person who is able to generate interest in something (such as a consumer product) by posting about it on social media

Sadly, in our celebrity-obsessed world, the second definition has taken over. It's rare now to hear the word "influencer" without "Instagram" or "social media" before it.

It's true that social media is one arena where you can have influence. But here's what's not true: If—and only if—you have a million followers then you automatically have influence.

That belief actually robs us of our power to be true influencers.

As the Beatles sang, "We all want to change the world." Another way of saying that is, "We want to leave the world a better place than it was when we arrived." *That's* the kind of influence most of us crave deeply.

So, a life of meaning and fulfillment doesn't come from getting a million people to buy something or give you "likes." It comes from knowing exactly what you want to improve in the world and helping set that change in motion.

Influence isn't a numbers game or a popularity contest. It isn't about simply spouting your opinions and preferences and getting others to imitate you. If you approach it that way, you actually diminish your capacity for influence.

When you develop true influence, you finally stop trying to prove that you matter because you *know* you do. You matter because you've become a disrupter to promote something better than the status quo.

You stop trying to please others and you allow yourself to be outrageously expressive as you propose new ideas—ideas that some insist are crazy and will never work.

You're willing to say the hard stuff many don't want to hear.

You stop thinking about yourself so much because you're determined to have an impact on a topic that's much bigger than you.

You don't hold yourself back out of fear or low self-esteem, and you don't self-aggrandize either. You also don't need endless praise and accolades to stay motivated. It's simply not about you anymore.

In short, you trade being mired in self-doubt for being propelled by a great big soul-driven purpose.

You just step up and do what you know needs to be done.

And how do you know what needs to be done?

True influencers generally have a vision or idea that seemed to come from beyond their usual level of thinking. Some feel it came from Source or their higher self. But it doesn't matter whether your mission as an influencer arrives in an unexpected flash or gradually dawns on you based on your life challenges.

What matters is that a true influencer's mission comes from a sense of deep connection to at least one of three things:

- People
- Animals
- Our planet

As an influencer, you're passionate about improving one or more of those things in a specific way. You don't just wish you could make things better. You decide what you want to make better and how, and then you go for it.

"Going for it" might involve becoming a widely-recognized leader—the person who takes center stage. But to be an influencer, you don't have to be the loudest voice in the room that persuades the masses. There are other ways influencers go for it, such as being the one who exerts quiet genius behind the scenes.

The word "influence" comes from the Latin, "in-fluere," which means "into flow." Influencers, whether behind the scenes or in the spotlight, point out where there's need for a new flow of ideas and actions. Rather than working to incrementally improve something that we're already doing, influencers help us move in a new direction. They tap into an evolution that wants to happen.

For example, Pam Fleischer of Twirl realized there's a fundamental flaw with the experience most women have giving birth. Typically, a pregnant woman checks into a hospital and immediately takes on all the trappings of a patient. And what do we associate with being a hospital patient? Primarily sickness, pain, and a sense of helplessness.

How different would it be if, at that magical time, a woman could feel less like a patient and more like a Goddess? What if she could experience a potent, even sensual sense of her own sexuality and power?

Pam realized that one major part of making that happen would be pregnant women wearing something other than the dreaded hospital gown. So, she created a much more attractive and comfortable outfit, which included a top and a birthing skirt—an outfit a woman could feel healthy and powerful in.

For several years she tried to get that outfit into hospitals. When she realized that was not going to work, she began introducing it to hypno-birthing circles and yoga classes for pregnant woman. In doing that, she helped build and influence a movement to empower pregnant women. She created demand and awareness by going around the blockage in the system, the medical establishment, and directly appealing to the people hungry for this change, the women getting ready to give birth.

Similarly, the organic food movement started when farmers realized the pesticides in our food were detrimental to consumers, growers, and the planet. Even though the use of these was subsidized by governments, which actually made it cheaper to produce and sell them, some farmers had had enough. Although there was little demand for funnier looking, more expensive fruits and veggies, some farmers began growing without toxic chemicals. At first, they could only sell them in farmer's markets and health food stores. Gradually though, awareness spread that these foods were not just much healthier but also tastier. As a result, today most major grocery stores have an organic section.

Yoga Tribe Mats was born when one woman realized that millions of yoga mats were sold every year, and they were all non-biodegradable. She wanted to create an environmentally friendly mat. Of course, with so many mats readily available, the idea of introducing another one hardly seemed like a sure-fire idea.

Then one day in meditation, a design came to her: a flower-of-life symbol that would appear on every mat. She was inspired and went for it. She was not primarily motivated by money, but the demand for these mats turned out to be extraordinary. Yogis everywhere loved the idea of bringing sustainability to the world of yoga. Soon, she was making the world better in a significant way and generating far more income than she could have imagined.

While money often comes to an influencer, a true influencer sees amassing money not as an end goal but as a tool to help facilitate change.

Tom's Shoes founder, Blake Mycoskie, took a trip to Argentina. There he met a woman who was distributing shoes to shoeless children. Being around her, he realized the serious health consequences for children not having shoes. And soon he had the idea to create a shoe company in North America that would, for each pair of shoes sold, send a free pair to a child in Argentina.

Today, the company generates billions. To make that happen, Blake committed to not just starting another shoe company but one with a dual commitment to creating a great product and to doing something great for the world. He knew a great product would generate great revenue, and with that revenue, he would do great things.

So, what's the great thing you want to do for the world?

Don't let your answer be clouded by concerns about whether it will work, whether the world is ready for it, or whether it will make money. If there's something you feel passionate about changing on this planet, then that's what you're on this planet to do.

You don't need to start a company or become famous. If either of those things are meant to happen, they will. But that's not your concern now. You will know what step to take all along the way, and be able to take it, as long as you get into the flow of being an influencer. And that starts with knowing what you want to do and then doing something about it.

Step 1 is to answer this question:

When I think about people, animals, or our planet…

If I let go of all concerns about outcome, or money, or being up to the challenge…

What, do I passionately want to make better?

(Be as specific as you can about the issue or challenge that gets you most fired up and what you think the solution is.)

CHAPTER 2

Ignite a spark, don't own the flame
To create a movement and leave a legacy, you need to be more concerned about the change you're making than the credit you're getting.

If you can imagine a better world, then you have important work to do here.

The twinge of pain you feel in the face of human or animal suffering…

That sense of disgust and outrage you experience observing the degradation of our planet…

These tell you you're meant to be an influencer. The ability and desire to start or help further a movement is encoded in your DNA.

Why, then, does it feel so challenging?

Ultimately, a movement is about birthing or promoting a set of values that differs from the prevailing values of your culture. The *result or goal* of a movement may be a change in the physical or material world, but the movement itself is a spiritual undertaking designed to up-level human consciousness.

All lasting, positive change is an outer reflection of an inner shift, and inner shift starts with you feeling a burning need for something to change. Then, you set out to ignite that same spark in others.

You can't attempt to own the flame because flame that's too still or contained goes out. Flame spreads by being in flow. And as an influencer, you don't manage the moment; you flow into the future. You must see yourself as passing the torch again and again until an overwhelming number of people feel the same inner burn as you.

Of course, that's challenging when we've been indoctrinated with the belief that if we have a good idea, the most important thing is that it brings us acclaim and money.

Yet, imagine if, for example, Martin Luther King Jr. had tried to "own" the civil rights movement. Even the idea is preposterous, isn't it? Instead, MLK believed that, "An individual has not started living until he can rise above the narrow confines of his individualistic concerns to the broader concerns of all humanity."

In the Western World today, with so many constantly worried about just making ends meet and a cultural fixation on personal gain and achievement, rising above our individualistic concerns takes effort and courage.

Recently, children and young adults, have been leading the way on this. Young people tend to be keenly aware they are inheriting a world they will inhabit for a while and then pass on. They are, therefore, typically more willing to question and challenge norms and more optimistic about their ability to influence change.

An inspiring recent example is Greta Thunberg, who, as an 11-year old suffering from depression, was diagnosed with Asperger's syndrome, Obsessive Compulsive Disorder, and selective mutism. At the age of 15, her distress over how little was being done to address climate change led her to protest outside the Swedish parliament. News of her action spread, and soon students inspired by Greta were protesting for stronger climate action in cities everywhere.

Rather than view her multiple diagnoses as limitations, Greta has called Asperger's her superpower and stated that having selective mutism means she only speaks when necessary.

At the age of 16, Greta published her collected speeches under the title, "No One Is Too Small to Make a Difference." And in 2019, Greta declared, "everyone out there, it is now time for civil disobedience. It is time to rebel."

MLK, Greta Thunberg, and virtually any world-changer you can think of took action not because they felt uniquely qualified nor because they sought fame and fortune. They took action because they knew in their bones that as Greta said, "it is now time."

At this particular moment, more and more of us are awakening to an urgent realization that it is now time. As President Barack Obama said, "We are the first generation to feel the effect of climate change and the last generation who can do something about it."

Knowing that is true—combined with an awareness of all the other challenges that seem to be boiling over in the world—can easily make you feel cynical and want to throw your hands up in despair.

Many people right now are feeling that kind of despair. But influencers play a different game—a game that will lead you, too, out of despair (or frustration and uncertainty about what to do) and into being an influencer.

In the last chapter, you began getting into the flow of being an influencer by answering the question: *What do I passionately want to make better?*

Once you know that, it's time to start playing the influencer game.

That means agreeing to live according to a couple guiding principles (which may not immediately thrill you). These principles are:

1. I chose everything I've been through—including all my personal challenges and even being alive on this planet at this particular moment—because there is something I'm meant to learn and teach.
2. Discovering and expressing what I'm meant to teach is my real purpose and far more important than any acclaim or fortune I could ever acquire.

Yes, the influencer game asks you to imagine that you are 100% responsible for your life … all of it.

Now, to play this game, you don't have to fully embrace or believe that you chose your parents and all your challenging circumstances as a learning experience. But you have to be willing to live *as if* you did, in the empowering way this perspective opens up to you. This can transform you from feeling like your life is a story of pain and hardship you're simply stuck with, to seeing it as a story of incredible discovery you are meant to share.

Notice that Greta Thunberg called Asperger's syndrome her superpower. That is a beautiful peek into the mind of an influencer and why some people can show up so powerfully.

Most of us are trapped in the "who am I to do this?" conversation. We see "influencers" online and in the media, and we think that to have influence, you need to check at least one of these boxes:

- Look like a supermodel
- Speak like a trained performer
- Be a genius who has built an empire
- Have extraordinary wealth (either created or inherited)

But world-changers like Greta Thunberg demonstrate you don't need any of those things to be powerfully influential. You just need to feel like a superhero with a superpower on the inside.

That feeling opens the door for you to embody a most critical influencer quality we identified in the previous chapter: The willingness to be outrageously expressive as you propose new ideas that some insist are crazy and will never work.

Doing that takes superhero-level courage.

To develop that courage, it helps to create a new image of yourself. So, the next time you need to express a powerful idea—whether to a small audience or a very large one—you don't just show up as you typically would. You show up as the superhero your life has been preparing you to be (probably without you noticing… until now!).

So, let's take the first step toward you showing up that way.

It's time do something that at first might seem more wacky than powerful but actually will help you show up in a powerful, new way.

It's time to imagine yourself as a cartoon character.

Think about and answer these questions:

If you had superpowers, what would they be?

If you had your exaggerated cartoon features, what would you look like?

If you had your cartoon character outfit on, what would you be wearing?

Allow yourself to go deeply into this cartoon character version of yourself. Think about the superpowers your life has given you and the ones you need to become the influencer you want to be.

Let yourself go over the top. Maybe you need to fly. Maybe you have a big necklace on that radiates magnetic information, and wearing it enables people from any part of the world to understand you. Maybe you have an amazing headdress on that allows you to do something else magical.

Spend some time on the questions above. By mentally going into your cartoon-character self, you will open to a level of expressiveness most of us have shut down. And being willing and able to be outrageously expressive is, itself, a superpower that will instantly build your influence.

To help you more easily and fully realize your cartoon-with-superpowers self, below is a guided visualization.

Discover Your Cartoon Character Visualization

(**Note:** To experience this visualization, have someone read it to you or record yourself reading it and then listen. Also, have a pen and pad of paper when you do it.)

Find a comfortable place to sit in an upright position where you won't be disturbed…

Close your eyes… take a deep breath in… and exhale through your mouth.

And as you start to sink into the chair, uncross your legs and your hands. Allow your body to become soft and heavy.

Take deep breath in… and exhale.

And as you're breathing in, you're breathing in energy… fresh energy… life force into every cell of your body. And as you're breathing out, you're breathing out any stress… any disappointment… any doubt.

And as you're breathing in again, breathe in into every cell of your body, bringing the energy into the back of the heart.

And as you're breathing out, breathe out any worries or thoughts of disappointment or resentment.

As you're breathing in again, breathe into the back of the heart, that area that stores stuck energy… and feel the life force and vitality entering your body.

And as you continue doing this, you're starting to feel that every cell in your body is vibrating with an effervescence of light. And any areas that feel dull or heavy, you just breathe into them… breathe some more light in, and then breathe out anything that's stuck or heavy.

Take several more breaths, breathing light in, and heaviness out…

[Pause here long enough for three deep breaths]

Now, I'd like you to go to a place in nature, which is your perfect nature spot. A place that brings life force to you.

It can be anywhere. It can be on a mountain… in front of the ocean… it can be in a forest, or on a desert. Find your place in nature that truly is your place.

And when you arrive there, feel how the body responds to just dropping this weight because you're in this truly beautiful, safe space, which is full of freedom and contentment.

As you look around at the colors in this space, notice that there's a 360-degree way that you can look around and see what's behind you and to the sides of you, and that you feel completely protected.

As you look down at your feet, which are bare on the earth, you notice the color and the texture of the earth.

Notice this beautiful texture...and maybe you can even pick up a scent in this beautiful nature spot.

Allow the air to just be on your skin...and notice that you are also naked...and that within this space you feel completely aligned.

Everything is attuned, and you feel really well looked after...

And now, I want you to imagine that you're going into a vast open space, almost like a blank canvas.

And in this space, imagine this is your cartoon and you are a cartoon character that appears on the screen in front of you.

So, the first thing about cartoons that I want to mention is that they are really two dimensional. They're really simple to understand.

So, exaggerate your qualities and imagine what you're wearing as this character. You can be anything, but what are you wearing?

And then exaggerate some of the features because cartoons are meant for children, and there are no repeat characters in the stories. In a cartoon, there's only one character with one role.

And then another character will come in and have a different role. So, you never cross over, and it's never confusing.

So, when you think about yourself as a cartoon character with your exaggerated stance, ask yourself, what does this cartoon character look like?

Is it a mythological kind?

Is it a comedy kind?

Is it a detective type of cartoon?

What is the genre of your character?

And then if we were to just go a little further… what is this cartoon character's superpower?

Superpowers are the thing that you need to explain to a child. It needs to be really visible.

So, for instance, my cartoon character is very much like this high priestess kind of image. So, it's mythological. I wear a crown on my head, which has the phases of the moon. And I have a necklace at my throat, which, my superpower is that I can speak to anything.

And so, as I appear on the screen, my priestess-y kind of character comes in. And when I'm active with my superpower, a beam that comes out of her necklace. And as that beam affects everybody around her or all the plants and animals, she is able to communicate with all of them, all of nature.

So, whatever it is that you do, you might have a tool as your character, you might carry something, you might have a head dress, you might have something that represents, when you pick it up or use it, that's when you activate your superpower.

Or, your superpower may just come straight through you. But the key with children is they need to see the effect of the superpower on the other characters.

So, ask yourself: How do we see your effect on the other characters with your superpower?

So, going back to my example, for me, when the beam of light radiates out from my necklace and goes all around me, then animals who are in the beam can speak to me directly. It can be kind of funny because it's a funny character as well. But it's also like suddenly the cats are speaking to me and you can see that they are mute, normal animals and then, all of a sudden, they will start speaking if the beam of light is on.

If another human character was around me when the beam of light was activated, then they would be able to express their deepest desires. It's as if they've been in a fog and then they're in my beam of light and all of a sudden, they've shaped themselves. That's the cartoon level.

You got to see the effect that you have. So, these characters shaped themselves and then they'll speak their desires. So, think about what it is that you do and how you affect people. Or you may affect the planet, or you may have some other kind of superpower.

Once you gather as much of this information as you can, you could even ask yourself, what are the qualities of this character?

How does this character dress?

What is this character's superpower? Is it more than one?

Does this character use a tool in order to activate the superpower?

And how can everybody else in that scene know that the superpower has occurred?

And then, when you're ready, now we're going to come out of this.

So, I'm just going to ask you to rub your hands together. Rub..rub.. rub… generate heat… rub hard.

Now place your palms over your closed eyes… breathe in… and exhale.

Now, rub your hands together again… rub… rub..rub…

Place them over your closed eyes, breathe in and exhale.

And then one more time … really rub your hands together hard and generate heat.

Place your palms over your closed eyes … breathe in … and exhale.

And then you can rub your hair back of the neck … temples … jaw … throat … forehead … and rub your face.

And then you can come back into the space … and open your eyes.

And now write down as quickly as you can everything that came to you about your cartoon character.

CHAPTER 3

A movement means always moving
It's called a movement because it's an evolution—a shift—not an end point.

To feel called to help people, animals, or the planet and not act on it, is to shut down part of yourself.

Many are in that shutdown state wondering why they are so unhappy.

On the other hand, to answer the call to act takes courage. And that courage is easier to have when you realize how simultaneously important and unimportant you are.

Scientists estimate there are around 30 billion planets in our galaxy and perhaps two trillion galaxies in the universe. In the scheme of things, our solar system is far less than a grain of sand. Somewhat humbling, isn't it? It can quickly take the wind out of your sails if you are focused on being "important."

Yet, you are important because you're part of the same movement that created all those galaxies and the planets and stars they contain. In fact, the odds of you being born were between 1 in 400 trillion and 1 in 400 quadrillion.

In other words, there was basically no chance of you ever existing. And yet, here you are! We all come from Source, are reflections of that Source, and therefore are hugely important.

By your very nature, you're part of a movement that is currently expressing as you. It's a movement of consciousness experiencing itself as form—and growing ever more aware and more conscious. And now you can only be completely fulfilled if you help drive that evolution of consciousness forward.

That means, when you become aware something needs changing and you take action, you feel amazing because you're being true to your nature. You are on purpose. But when you know something needs changing and you do nothing, your esteem and happiness take a hit because you have betrayed yourself. You are off purpose.

It's easy to get confused about this in a world where strong forces entice us to fit in, get what's ours, and accept the status quo. But to understand the fallacy of that approach to life, just think about the values and norms that governed the lives of your grandparents or great grandparents.

What opportunities and comforts do you enjoy that were unavailable to someone like you only a couple of generations ago? And how many of those are thanks to some kind of forward movement in either consciousness, technology, or both that pierced the status quo?

From the moment of our birth to the moment of our last breath, we *are* movement—and we're designed to help humanity flow into the future a bit more conscious and humane. Because we exist within, and as part, of a movement, nothing we endeavor to influence has an ending.

This is obvious when we think of the movement of technology. For example, consider photography. It was invented in the early 1800s. For a while, cameras were huge, photos were low quality, and developing a print could take several days. By the mid 20th Century, people could carry small point-and-click cameras that instantly produced photos. Today, we have phones that take digital photos with amazing clarity and detail. And who can imagine what we'll have years from now? Perhaps instruments as thin as a credit card and small enough to fit in the palm of your hand that produce holograms.

The same kind of evolution happens with social movements. For example, consider the battle for gay rights. In 1969, the Stonewall riot was a fight to end the arrests of gay people in the United States simply for gathering where they could be openly gay. Forty-six years, and many battles later—including hard-won fights over legal discrimination and the AIDS crisis—The Supreme Court of the United States legalized gay marriage. By that time, a majority of the public supported it. Yet, legal and social battles for LGBQT rights as parents, employees, and in many other areas continue.

While technology often moves forward in a series of thrilling leaps (even if the leaps sometimes have negative ramifications), social movements tend to involve heartbreaking setbacks, acts of bravery, and societal growing pains as one group expresses pain or outrage while another defends the old order.

Ultimately, social change happens when enough hearts and minds experience a shift so that former defenders of the status quo are willing to follow or get out of the way. Historically, movements often start with angry activists who bring the problem to light in a way that makes it impossible for society at large to ignore. A great example is the 2019 Extinction Rebellion demonstrations all over Europe that were done to highlight our environmental crisis. They occupied major thoroughfares for two weeks at a time, shutting down traffic and stopping business.

But once activists create widespread awareness, the world needs influencers to help large numbers of people have a shift in thinking so they actually want to make a change, even if they don't see an immediate, personal gain from it.

It's through the power of emotional connection that true influencers motivate others to do things like conserve water, give up plastic, change to a more planet-friendly diet, or change public policies. The great gift of an influencer is to help others see and feel the pain of not making a change, and the inner or outer reward of making one, without making them feel wrong.

When you can offer something new and make what you're proposing feel beneficial even to people who have benefitted from the old way, you are an influencer. The ability to do that comes from a lot of inner work, especially around channeling anger in a positive way.

How do you learn to do that?

Buddhism emphasizes eight practices for ending ignorance that are the ideal influencer formula:

- Right Speech
- Right View
- Right Intention
- Right Action
- Right Livelihood
- Right Effort
- Right Mindfulness
- Right Concentration

When you consciously and diligently work to practice each of these while committing yourself to a movement that comes from your heart, you WILL be an influencer.

As an influencer, there are movements you start and movements you join or inherit.

It goes like this:

You feel called to act and know that now is the time. Then…

If you know what to do, you do it.

If you don't know what to do, you align yourself with someone who does.

Chief Seattle is credited with saying, "When the earth is sick, the animals will disappear, when that happens, The Warriors of the Rainbow will come to save them."

There is some controversy about the accuracy of that quote and the origins of The Rainbow Prophecy. But the sentiment is that when the earth is in trouble, the right people will show up and come together to inspire the necessary transformation.

Right now, many are showing up for that.

How will you show up?

How will you use this 1 in 400 quadrillion chance you have to be part of ensuring that people like you, generations from now, will have all the opportunities you have and more that we can't even imagine yet?

If that question feels daunting, what could you do just to make life a little better in some way for someone else right now?

Consider the following questions:

Is there an action I'm called to take or a business I want to start?

Or, is it time to align with someone who already has a movement?

What movement is happening right now that I feel passionate about?

What person or organization is leading the way on it?

How can I align myself with them and contribute to the solution they're offering?

CHAPTER 4

It's not the result, it's the evolution
A movement isn't about immediate results; it's about the evolution you inspire.

Without a mission that feels bigger than you, you constantly wonder, "How can I make myself good enough for the world to give me the love, safety, and recognition I crave?"

When you have a mission bigger than yourself, the question becomes, "How do I help make the world a bit better at giving all living things the love, safety, and recognition they need."

The first question creates a life of seeking but never finding. That's great for getting us to buy things to fill an inner void, but it's not so great for experiencing happiness.

The second question leads to happiness and self-love simply as a side effect of knowing we're making a meaningful difference.

To fully give ourselves over to a movement in this way, we have to know that it is our commitment, not our results, that matter.

Another way of saying this is, to be a true influencer, you have to be somewhat irrational. You have to put more trust in your vision of what's possible than in what appears likely right now.

In prehistoric times, people had an easier time of this. They saw Spirit in nature and devoted themselves to herculean tasks that seemed impossible. A great illustration of this is Stonehenge. We don't know the exact purpose of the site. But we do know it was aligned to the sun and stars, was a temple where people gathered for ceremony, and had huge spiritual significance. The building of it happened over thousands of years and involved monumental effort to move incomprehensibly heavy stones long distances without any system of wheels and pulleys.

Many people devoted themselves to one small part of the task of building Stonehenge—and those tasks often took hundreds of years to complete. Unlike many other Neolithic achievements, Stonehenge does not appear to have involved forced labor of any kind.

So, what compelled them to keep going?

They must have instinctively known something we've forgotten: Our only significance comes from being part of the whole. Back before there were photos, film, or written records, there was essentially no hope of being remembered for very long as an individual. But everyone lived the same fundamental hero's journey we live today.

It's the journey we love to see in movies and read about in books. Every movie, every book, and every life basically tells of the same journey: The hero encounters incredible obstacles and adversity. She feels like giving up, but she doesn't. She believes in the seemingly impossible, and she winds up with a new wisdom and strength. Usually, in some way, she's gone beyond her own limitations and self-absorption and opened to giving and receiving something greater.

It's that inner change in the hero that makes a story—or a life—deeply meaningful.

And it's the way we, in our own hero's journey, devote ourselves to something, handle adversity, and grow in the process, that makes the story of our life as deeply meaningful as any hero in history or fiction.

That's why it's better to dedicate yourself to an ideal that may never be reached than to accept a current reality you know could be better.

As an influencer, you inspire an evolution by committing to your own evolvement rather than settling for a false sense of safety. You recognize that the ideal you imagine—while it may not be achievable—contains a level of truth that our less-than-ideal world lacks. The "what we could be" picture you have in your head becomes more honest than accepting the idea that "what is" represents the best we can do.

So, you bring the truth, and Spirit brings the timetable. The change you seek to inspire may happen within a decade, in 100 years, or be an ideal humanity will always be striving for. But the important thing for you is that you spoke your truth, you lived your truth, and you evolved in the process.

If your desire is to build a business as an influencer with a movement, it is harder to accept that it's your commitment and not your results that matter. A business needs to make money. But equally important is that, if you are an influencer, you will never feel satisfied with a business (or a job) that you're in exclusively for the money. So, the question for you will always be, how can I have a business that makes money AND makes a difference. The answer to that always starts with looking at what you're doing now or what's happening in the industry you're interested in and asking, "What's the evolution that needs to happen and how can I inspire it?"

Whether you're starting a movement or joining one. Whether you're devoting your free time to being an influencer or building a business around it, you need to unplug and detach from all the negativity around us. You need to let go of the messages in your head telling you what isn't possible.

To do lightwork, you need to deprogram from self-doubt, pessimism, and cynicism.

We live in a cynical time. But it's our belief in the darkness that makes these times seem so dark.

How does it feel if I tell you that this dark time on our planet is leading up to a Golden Age? Does that sound possible? Or, do you think: "Are you f★★★★ing kidding me? Open your eyes! We're going to destroy the planet!"

In Chapter 2 I said that to be an influencer you don't have to 100% believe that you chose your parents and all the circumstances of your life, but you have to be willing to live *as if* you did.

The same is true about the idea that we're moving into a Golden Age. You don't have to 100% believe that it's a given. But you have to think and behave *as if* it's going to happen and you're here to help bring it about.

When you really think about it, even if ocean levels are rising and the climate is changing, we still have the ability to profoundly affect what life will be like for future generations. We can leave a legacy that leads to them fighting for scraps, or one that leads them to experiencing love and compassionate solutions that work for all despite the challenges they inherited.

What if the next Golden Age is all about an inner shift humanity needs, and our outer challenges are the very thing we need to make the change from running on fear and selfishness to running on love?

Now THAT would be an evolution!

Want to help bring it on?

Consider the following questions:

To be an influencer, what thought(s) do I need to let go of about what's possible?

What self-doubts do I need to release?

What story about the future of humanity and our planet do I need to question?

What would I really like to believe about what our future could be?

When I imagine a Golden Age for humanity, what do I see?

What's one thing (big or small) I could do to make that vision of a Golden Age more likely?

Am I willing to do that thing?

When?

CHAPTER 5

You can do it "wrong" if your stand is strong!
A profound stand is more important than any positioning or marketing.

Do you feel called to develop a business as an influencer?

If you do, you will become a special kind of influencer... and a special kind of entrepreneur.

Being in business as an influencer is different from simple activism. As an activist, you may do something you don't particularly enjoy in order to create a result you want. For example, you might go door-to-door canvassing to save a river. You don't necessarily love canvassing, but you're willing to do it for a period of time to get the job done.

In contrast, when you start a business as an influencer, you need to marry what you feel passionate about changing with something you love to do. In other words, your goal isn't just to create a change—it's to create a change *by doing something you love.*

Sometimes, that can lead you in directions that at first sound crazy. But when you uncover a deep, genuine need, you can succeed no matter how crazy it sounds. That's called discovering your super niche, and when you do, you have a pre-existing market with no competition.

For example, a woman named Silvia realized that her love was holding babies. Her stand was that we generally serve parents at birth and when they have toddlers, but there's a time in between when we drop them. That's the time when their babies need to be held constantly. It's also the time when overwhelm can be greatest and post-natal depression becomes a serious issue.

Silvia loved holding babies, and she saw that there is a time when parents need support doing that more than anything else. For new mothers and fathers, just having someone trustworthy to hold their baby could alleviate huge stress and create tremendous freedom.

Another part of her stand was honesty. Silvia wanted parents to be able to be honest about how challenging the earliest stages of parenting can be. So, there was no need to put on a happy face around her. She would speak directly into the pains of being new parents, and parents could talk honestly about this with her as she held their babies.

Today, Silvia has a successful baby-holding business that's meaningful and brings her joy.

You might wonder how you could ever market something as unusual as holding babies. But marketing a business with a mission is different from marketing one that just sells something or offers a service. You don't need the perfect marketing or positioning because the authenticity of your passion and the authentic need for what you offer speak for themselves.

Sharon Gannon and David Life, the founders of Jivamukti yoga, are great examples of this. Their passion is spiritual activism with a particular interest in veganism and animal rights. To become influencers in that sphere, they created a whole system of yoga, which they loved doing. Based on three lineages that are each 5,000 years old, their system leads to transformation by awakening the spiritual activist in people, so they eat, show up, and interact differently in the world.

Sharon and David opened a yoga studio in 1984 that featured pictures of animal abuse in the hallway. And they marketed themselves using photos in which they look more like extremely eccentric performance artists than traditional yoga teachers, being they were part of the New York art scene. Yet, what they offered was in a class of its own and, despite their messaging, which any ad agency would no doubt consider all wrong, theirs is now the fastest-growing form of yoga on the planet. The key was their authenticity. Their business is now worth millions and is a highly respected form of yoga teacher training.

Again, the secret to that kind of success lies in creating a business doing something you love in service of your strongest stand. Of course, you need great clarity about your strongest stand, what you love to do, and how these two things can come together. So, let's take you through a process to help with that now.

Core Values and Top Passions Visualization

The visualization below uncovers your top three core values, your top three passions, and how you can interweave them. It has led numerous people to unexpected realizations about what they're really here to do.

(**Note:** To experience this visualization, have someone read it to you or record yourself reading it and then listen. Also, have a pen and pad of paper when you do it.)

Find a comfortable place to sit in an upright position where you won't be disturbed…

Close your eyes… take a deep breath in… and exhale through your mouth.

And as you start to sink into the chair, uncross your legs and your hands. Allow your body to become soft and heavy.

Take deep breath in… and exhale.

And as you're breathing in, you're breathing in energy…fresh energy…life force into every cell of your body. And as you're breathing out, you're breathing out any stress…any disappointment…any doubt.

And as you're breathing in again, breathe in into every cell of your body, bringing the energy into the back of the heart.

And as you're breathing out, breathe out any worries or thoughts of disappointment or resentment.

As you're breathing in again, breathe into the back of the heart, that area that stores stuck energy…and feel the life force and vitality entering your body.

And as you continue doing this, you're starting to feel that every cell in your body is vibrating with an effervescence of light. And any areas that feel dull or heavy, you just breathe into them…breathe some more light in, and then breathe out anything that's stuck or heavy.

Take several more breaths, breathing light in, and heaviness out…

[Pause here long enough for three deep breaths]

Now, I'd like you to go to a place in nature, which is your perfect nature spot. A place that brings life force to you.

It can be anywhere. It can be on a mountain…in front of the ocean…it can be in a forest, or on a desert. Find your place in nature that truly is your place.

And when you arrive there, feel how the body responds to just dropping this weight because you're in this truly beautiful, safe space, which is full of freedom and contentment.

As you look around at the colors in this space, notice that there's a 360-degree way that you can look around and see what's behind you and to the sides of you, and that you feel completely protected.

As you look down at your feet, which are bare on the earth, you notice the color and the texture of the earth.

Notice this beautiful texture…and maybe you can even pick up a scent in this beautiful nature spot.

Allow the air to just be on your skin…and notice that you are also naked…and that within this space you feel completely aligned.

Everything is attuned, and you feel really well looked after.

So now we're going to move to a very happy memory.

And I want you to go to a memory where it may have been many years ago when you were a child, or it could even be just last week.

But as you go to this happy memory, I want you to focus on the details.

So, notice where you were…

And if you were with anybody, home in on that detail. Notice the smaller, little things that you might see. It might be somebody's hands, or it might be a detail on somebody's face.

And then I want you to feel in your body, what is it like when you're happy?

Now, imagine that what you're looking at is like a virtual postcard.

These postcards that we pull out from our life…these wonderful memories that we can pull out every now and then.

So, you're able to step into this memory and feel the feelings of what it's like, those timeless moments.

And as you feel that feeling in your body, notice if there's anything different about the way you are.

Now notice if, for instance, your jaw is more relaxed… your shoulders are more relaxed.

Notice what it feels like when you can just relax… where there's nothing to do and nowhere to go.

You're completely in tune with your environment.

And then, as if you could turn a video camera on yourself, I want you to imagine what you look like when you're truly happy.

So now I'm going to ask you the first question from this place, and I want you to experience it like it bubbles up, not like you think have to think about it. Just allow this to just bubble up.

So, the first question is: What are your three core values?

[Pause for a few seconds]

And now I want you to put them in order.

So, the top core value, what is that?

And then the second…

And then the third…

Now, I'd like you to quickly your eyes and just write down those core values one after another in order.

And when you have them, close your eyes again, and take a deep breath in... and exhale.

And you find yourself back in that beautiful nature spot.

And as you relax back into it, and you're breathing with every cell in your body, so much connection that you even feel with every cell in your body that you're breathing in nature... you're becoming one with nature.

And then once again, you reach for the dial, which allows you to turn up the saturation of the color.

So, turn the dial and allow the vividness of the colors in this scene to come through for you.

And then I'd like you to also consider if there's anything you can hear in this beautiful nature scene.

Maybe you can pick up a scent on the wind.

So, taking a deep breath again, I want you to just go back to that beautiful memory when you were truly happy.

And once again, just feel yourself in that place, which was just a beautiful experience for you.

Timeless.

And notice some of the detail of what is going on in this scene...

And then notice what your body feels like as you drop into this scene.

And then, as if we could turn a video camera on you again, I want you to notice what your face looks like.

Is your skin shiny? Are your eyes sparkling?

Because when we're in those places where we're truly happy, there's nowhere to go. It's total connection.

And so, I'm going to ask you the second question, and this can have the context of a project or a business or next level of business that you're interested in. Or, it can just simply be something that you love doing.

So, the question is: What are your three key passions?

And once again, I want you to put these in order.

So, even if they all seem important, I want you to decipher which is the top key passion for you.

And now, I'd like you to gently open your eyes again and write down those top three key passions one after another in order.

[Pause for a few seconds]

When you've done that, close your eyes again.

Now, what is the top core value with the top key passion?

Those two words or two sentences or phrases will be the structure and essence of your super-nice right there. If you had to think you would be doing these things for the rest of your life, you know you would be happy.

The second thing I want you to observe is, this is the beginning of a very strong message.

And that these words will give you access to honing in on a certain skill that you are going to be talking about.

If you need to change the words, you keep the same frequency of the words. So, I'll give you an example. A client I worked with had "abundance" as one of her words. But because she was working in food and nutrition, she changed that word to "nourished" in her messaging.

When I had "abundance" in the work I was doing, I changed the word to "millionaire."

It has to have the same resonance but be completely unique and authentic to what you are up to.

The second piece of this exercise is, I want you to think of the other four words. So, think of the other two core values and the other two passions.

And what that will show you is the quality of what you can create this into.

So, they will be key parts of the message, almost like one is a header and those below will be the how I do this… how I create this… how I land it.

Often, it'll show you something like, you could be an events organizer where you organize an event which has certain qualities, for example.

So, can you see the connections between the four other words that you've put down?

[Pause for a few seconds]

Okay, great…

And now we're going to come out of this by rubbing your hands together, keeping your eyes shut.

And then place your hands over your closed eyes, breathe in and exhale.

Then you can rub your hairline…your face…the throat…back of the neck, just coming back into this space…and just allow yourself to arrive.

CHAPTER 6

Building a business that's a blessing
How to turn your existing business into a power center of influence by doing good deeds.

Not all of us have power, but we all have influence. That is why we can each be leaders. The most important forms of leadership come not with position, title or robes of office, not with prestige and power, but with the willingness to work with others to achieve what we cannot do alone; to speak, to listen, to teach, to learn, to treat other people's views with respect even if they disagree with us, to explain patiently and cogently why we believe what we believe and do what we do; to encourage others, praise their best endeavors and challenge them to do better still. Always choose influence rather than power. It helps change people into people who can change the world.

Power works by division, influence by multiplication. Power, in other words, is a zero-sum game: the more you share, the less you have. Influence is a non-zero game: the more you share, the more you have.

—Rabbi Lord Jonathan Sacks

The quotes above contrast power with influence. If you have a successful business, you are uniquely positioned to marry power with influence and, in the process, help redefine both business and power.

In our last chapter, we discussed creating a business doing something you love in service of your strongest stand. But what if you already have a successful business that's focused on something other than the difference you want to make?

For example, what if you are making widgets, and you want to do something about the death of coral reefs?

In that case, the big question to ask is, "Am I enjoying myself in my current business?" If your answer is no, then it's time to let go of what you're doing and create a new business that feels more meaningful and better aligned with your values.

If you answer, "Yes, I am enjoying myself," it's time to up your happiness even more by exploring how you can take the power that comes with your business and turn it into influence. Your role may not be to play the disrupter or the visionary when it comes to solving the problem you want solved. But you can play a vital role in empowering the person(s) or organization(s) playing that role.

In that case, the second question to ask yourself is, "How do I want to be of influence?" It could be purely by giving money. Given the current structure of our world, that's an important and vital way to drive change. For example, the company, Sevenly, sells clothing and accessories and gives a percentage of all their proceeds to one of seven causes ranging from autism to social justice.

Or, maybe for you it's primarily about getting involved in mentoring or education around an issue—perhaps an issue with a tie-in to the product or service you provide. For example, the eyeglass company, Warby Parker, donates a pair of eyeglasses for each pair purchased and trains people in developing countries to give basic eye exams.

As a business owner, you are ideally positioned to create a circle of influence by raising awareness about an issue and creating buy-in from other business owners. Often, the pure visionary and disrupter faces challenges getting business owners to listen and contribute to the effort. Visionaries can generally speak with urgency about their issue but aren't necessarily adept at addressing the resistance business owners may have to getting involved.

The way our culture has thought about success in business up to now has led most people with businesses to carefully guard their time, money, and energy. They've been conditioned to be laser focused on profit. The bottom line is beating the competition and rising to the top of the industry, whatever it takes. Even if you are part of a new breed of heart-centered, soul-focused entrepreneurs (thankfully, there are more and more of us emerging), this old paradigm still affects you. It's the reason so many who are in business to do great, humanitarian things still experience more stress than happiness and fulfillment.

So, when the issue you want to influence isn't the focus of your business, yet you want to turn your business into a power center for good by doing good deeds around that issue, you have to consciously shift into a new business paradigm. This is the paradigm that holds Success, with a capital "S," as requiring some form of giving back that creates a positive ripple in the world. This is the essence of marrying power with influence. It's a paradigm shift that will transform business and the business owners who get on board.

The concept of money and employment was a replacement for slavery. Today, in much of the world, the very idea of slavery seems outrageous, immoral, and unthinkable. Now, for the continued survival of the human species, we need to reach the point where we have the same feeling and perspective about amassing wealth and power merely for personal gain and aggrandizement.

Business owners who have awakened to this paradigm shift have an obligation to answer the call—and to share it with others in business. The era of exclusively numbers-based, time-bound business goals is quickly coming to an end. In addition to growth and profits, we now need to include goals pertaining to our own happiness and wellbeing. That sounds like a recipe for even more self-absorption … until we recognize that both of those things come from giving to others.

Indeed, if your ultimate goal is to look back on your life and feel it was well lived, you need to know and act on what will get you there. And the biggest factor that seems to put a smile on the face of people on their death bed is this: knowing they made a difference for others.

Once you let that sink in, annual growth and revenue goals—while necessary for a sustainable business—are hardly enough to keep you motivated … or, even once met, the key to feeling celebratory at year's end. That comes from the internal reward of knowing you did something positive for either people, animals, or the planet.

No matter what your business is, as someone with a successful business, you can change lives. And in the new paradigm, you're only truly successful when you do that.

Does your journey as an influencer involve turning your business into a power center of influence?

If it does, consider these questions:

What is the issue around which I feel most passionate about positioning myself as an influencer?

If it's an issue that has no inherent connection to the business you own, ask yourself: How would I like to have influence (giving money, mentoring, raising awareness, etc.)?

If you don't have an issue in mind yet, or there are several of interest to you, ask yourself: Is there an issue related to the business I have that I could get involved in? Is there something that would be a natural fit? What kind of influence could my business have here (giving something away, raising money, training, etc.)?

Once you have an issue in mind and a plan for how to channel your power as a business owner to influence it, ask, "What is my next step (is there a leader or organization you need to contact, a letter you need to write, etc.)?

And once you know your next step, take it!

CHAPTER 7

Leaving a legacy
Secrets of driving a movement that outlives you.

What does *legacy* really mean?

Marketing and sales copy often use the expression *leaving a legacy* to mean *giving others a reason to remember your name after you're gone.*

But striving to be remembered by name beyond the grave isn't the true definition of legacy. That's just a misguided idea coming from an ego wanting to preserve its own self-importance.

The real reason to care about your legacy is this: Even if you don't care, you leave one.

The choices you make and actions you take will be felt by others long after you're gone.

Right now, the legacy we're collectively on track to leave future generations is flooding, droughts, food shortages, dead oceans, and mass extinctions.

How different would our legacy look if we followed the Iroquois tradition of focusing on our impact seven generations ahead?

In our absence of doing that, by default, most of us are leaving a destructive, negative legacy.

Leaving a positive legacy is really about a transformation in consciousness from self-interest to shared interest and then taking actions from that place.

It's a commitment to leaving our planet better than it was when you arrived here.

And yet, legacy isn't primarily about figuring out what will be best in the future. It's about consistently thinking and acting in the best interest of whatever or whoever is in front of you right now ... whether that's another person, an animal, or some small corner of our world.

In Chapter 2, we said that the influencer game asks you to live as if you are 100% responsible for your life.

The legacy game asks you to live as if you are 100% responsible for everyone else's wellbeing starting now and going forward through multiple generations.

In case you feel resistant to this idea, note that this doesn't mean you are responsible for their feelings or choices.

Here's a helpful analogy. In business, excellent managers who lead high-functioning teams focus on this: Creating the conditions for employees to love their work.

These managers aren't responsible for how their employees perform. But they are 100% responsible for creating the conditions where every employee has the opportunity to function in their zone of genius, feel valued, connected, and have a great time.

Similarly, leaving a positive legacy means taking 100% responsibility for creating the conditions where this and future generations (as well as animals and our planet) can thrive.

From this shared-interest perspective, you know that every child is your child. Every country is your country. Every challenge is your challenge.

Which means that everything you do matters. Everything you say matters. And even everything you think matters.

Quantum physics shows us that all matter in the physical universe, including human beings, is made up of energy.

What we do with that energy literally impacts and shapes the lived experience of all beings now and in the future.

This is most clearly seen in family dynamics. The environment of abuse, abandonment, and heartache, or the environment of love, security, and compassion that parents create becomes part of a family's DNA. This is why many of us are currently working to transcend emotional coding that goes back hundreds or even thousands of years.

That we are living in a time of challenges like environmental devastation and a global pandemic leaves us with a daunting but thrilling choice. We can let our legacy be written for us, which means continuing to live as humans typically always have and helping usher in the eventual demise of humanity.

Or, we can assume the role of lightworkers, forgiving and releasing the past and ushering in a new chapter where humans live in harmony with each other, animals, and the planet.

That might sound like pure fantasy given our history and the moment of history we're presently living through. But at this point, living as if humanity will achieve that new and better chapter, and striving to make it happen, is the essence of leaving a positive legacy—and truly the essence of a life well lived.

In business, this means moving beyond just being concerned about profits and doing something that gives back…something of lasting value.

A great example is the company, Lizzie Outside. After facing her own mortality with a cancer diagnosis at 26, Lizzie Carr left her corporate job to pursue experiences that gave her a sense of meaning and purpose and made her feel alive. For her, that meant spending time in nature.

Following those interests led her to building the company and brand Lizzie Outside around being an author, activist, and adventurer. Today, she paddleboards the world and leads retreats while fighting plastic and pollution and helping others make more eco-friendly choices.

Lizzie is a perfect illustration of how recognizing that your time may be limited can motivate you to simultaneously make the most of every moment while thinking beyond your own narrow self-interest.

The bottom line is, knowing our time on the planet is limited can make us feel scared and unimportant, which leads to endless attempts to prove how much we matter. This leads to a life of pain and a legacy of simply adding to human suffering.

Alternatively, knowing our time is limited can make us feel a thrill that our true identity is as one small manifestation of all of life. We can realize that while our name will probably be forgotten, how we live and what we do matters more than we will ever know.

Most of us will not be personally remembered for long. But we will be felt. And that is a beautiful thing.

Let our great legacy be that in a time of rampant darkness, we chose to reach for the light.

When fear seemed to be spreading like a virus, we chose love.

That would be a legacy worth having.

What will that look like in your life?

CHAPTER 8

Your Sacred Pact
Committing to be the person you're meant to be and bring your vision into the world.

We said earlier that answering the inner call to help people, animals, or the planet takes courage. It also takes discipline and commitment.

Saying the unpopular thing...

Forgoing a sure source of income because it isn't aligned with your values...

Deeply engaging with the pressing issues of our time rather than chasing constant pleasure and comfort...

Doing business in a way that many people tell you won't work...

Those things are not easy.

So, how do you stay aligned with what matters most to your heart and not get seduced by the pull of self-absorption and instant gratification?

The answer is something called a "Sacred Pact." This is your code of conduct that brings your most authentic self and most meaningful vision into the world.

Consider how a computer is able to fulfill its function because it has an operating system that tells it how to behave—how to interact with and respond to programs, applications, user input, and so on.

Like a computer, you will create the conditions to fulfill your function by having an operating system known as your Sacred Pact. But this isn't a bunch of zeros and ones that set strict parameters on what you can do.

Rather, it's your declaration of the values you commit to embody and the change you know you're here to help usher in. It guides both what you do and who you'll be as you do it.

Will it limit or define who you are in every moment?

No.

It will illuminate who you aspire to show up as…grow into…discover yourself to be.

Growing into that person, through your daily and moment-to-moment choices, becomes your life's work.

And doing that work—that internal and external work—turns your experience here into a joyous classroom. It's a classroom where making a positive impact in the world and being true to yourself become one and the same.

So, how do you create your Sacred Pact?

You do it effortlessly through the visualization below, which allows your Sacred Pact to emerge spontaneously.

Sacred Pact Visualization
(**Note:** To experience this visualization, have someone read it to you or record yourself reading it and then listen.)

Find a comfortable place to sit in an upright position where you won't be disturbed…

Close your eyes… take a deep breath in… and exhale through your mouth.

And as you start to sink into the chair, uncross your legs and your hands. Allow your body to become soft and heavy.

Take deep breath in… and exhale.

And as you're breathing in, you're breathing in energy… fresh energy… life force into every cell of your body. And as you're breathing out, you're breathing out any stress… any disappointment… any doubt.

And as you're breathing in again, breathe in into every cell of your body, bringing the energy into the back of the heart.

And as you're breathing out, breathe out any worries or thoughts of disappointment or resentment.

As you're breathing in again, breathe into the back of the heart, that area that stores stuck energy… and feel the life force and vitality entering your body.

And as you continue doing this, you're starting to feel that every cell in your body is vibrating with an effervescence of light. And any areas that feel dull or heavy, you just breathe into them… breathe some more light in, and then breathe out anything that's stuck or heavy.

Take several more breaths, breathing light in, and heaviness out…

[Pause here long enough for three deep breaths]

Now, I'd like you to go to a place in nature, which is your perfect nature spot. A place that brings life force to you.

It can be anywhere. It can be on a mountain… in front of the ocean… it can be in a forest, or on a desert. Find your place in nature that truly is your place.

And when you arrive there, feel how the body responds to just dropping this weight because you're in this truly beautiful, safe space, which is full of freedom and contentment.

As you look around at the colors in this space, notice that there's a 360-degree way that you can look around and see what's behind you and to the sides of you, and that you feel completely protected.

As you look down at your feet, which are bare on the earth, you notice the color and the texture of the earth.

Notice this beautiful texture… and maybe you can even pick up a scent in this beautiful nature spot.

Allow the air to just be on your skin… and notice that you are also naked… and that within this space you feel completely aligned.

Everything is attuned, and you feel really well looked after.

So now we're going to go through a bit of a journey…

Imagine this is your sacred space, and there are some things that you'd like to bring into this sacred space.

So, creating a circle in this beautiful sacred space, imagine yourself in a sacred circle that you have created. In each quarter you have a representation of the different elements.

You have one that represents air: incense billowing in the wind.

And you have one that represents fire: you have a blazing fire in that quarter. And the warmth and the heat as you turn toward it makes you melt with comfort.

As you turn to the west, which is the site of water, there's a body of water in that direction and you feel a deep heart connection to the water itself… that feeling of freedom as you look over an ocean or a river or a pond, whichever it is.

And as you turn to the final quarter, the final element, it is earth. And you see a beautiful ancient crystal standing stone. It's been there so long and been part of many sacred circles. You look at the colors on this crystal and feel the age of it. It has been a witness to so many sacred pacts.

And standing in this circle, in the perfect nature element and in your sacred space, you are bringing in the energy now of ultimate truth for yourself.

So, allow the blessing of truth to be upon you as you realize that in this space, I can speak my truth, and in this space, I can say anything, and I will be protected.

So, the first part of the sacred pact is speaking that which you are here to do, and you're speaking to Great Spirit to Higher Self to Source. You're not speaking to partners or friends or family.

This is you speaking on why you're here and here's some of the words that bubble up when you're speaking at this level. This is declaration. I am.

Imagine that these truthful words spill from your tongue. And you're speaking into existence the very things that you are here to do as a frequency, as an energy, as somebody who is bringing legacy and healing on this planet...

Choosing 100% to be here, not making excuses for anything but saying, "I am!"

And think: who are you in this instance?

What are you here to do?

You can think of some of the biggest concepts, and you could even think of some of the smaller ones: I am... I am here for a life of love.

Whatever you notice coming up for you, allow these words to just flow out because you are speaking a truth. And then ask yourself, what are you here to do in this incarnation? What did you come here to do?

If there was a thread of legacy and what you are leaving different when you go on your journey, what is it that you are here to do?

What are you here to do *now*?

Because the energy of now brings a different energy and a different commitment. You may be somebody who's here to live in the country and be in nature and you're living in a city.

So, allow your truths to flow through you and add in the piece of now.

And then moving into a different conversation, allow yourself to imagine a code of conduct that is your operating system. That at the highest, highest level, you're taking an oath to self in the sacred circle about how you will *behave* on your journey.

How will you behave on your journey?

As you create the life of the things that you meant to do, what is the code of conduct in the way that you will deliver the things that you're meant to do?

So, if you are a leader, are you a generous leader? Is generosity important to you? If so, how would you show that you are operating from complete, 100% integrity at the level of sacred pack to self.

And then if you are a generous, are you generous to yourself? Because if you can't be generous to self, then you won't be teaching it fully and bringing it to the world.

So, code of conduct talks about not just how you behave toward others, but how you deliver your legacy. But how you also deliver to yourself.

This will pull up your socks abruptly if you are saying, I am generous and then you notice you're not, you know there's, there's something out of tune here. So, if your legacy is to speak up for the truth and then you shut down around the truth, then you're out of alignment.

And the final question is, "Who do I have to be to deliver my sacred pact?"

So, it's not just what are you here to do and how do you have to behave to be in integrity with this. It's also who do you have to be at the cellular level on the planet.

If you came to deliver a great message to people and your method was to use humor, then you know that you're out of integrity if you're not using humor and being playful to deliver it. If you're stern, if you're controlling, if you're harsh in your words, if you're not kind, then you're out of integrity with it.

So, feel into this space of who do I need to be to deliver and be completely in attunement with your message, with your operating system, with your path. And then allow yourself to ask in sacred space if there's anything else that you need to know about the Great Work that you're here to do.

And see if there's something that you are not fulfilling on and notice the discordant way that your body might respond, or an element might be out of attunement. And allow that information to go in because there are repercussions in not living the life that gives you life.

And that's the final part of the sacred pact--honoring yourself.

So, gathering all this information together, imagine that you could write these things into a manuscript as a statement of *I am… I am here to do this.*

I will behave in this way. I will be this kind of person. I will be this way around other people in this way.

And then finally, what is my highest level of honor to self?

And imagine that you wrote that down in lightning speed, and you roll this scroll back up, and you take it to the center of the circle that you're standing in. And you hold it like an oath. And this is the level of integrity that you will have with self, with others, with the way that you live your life and with your life force.

And as you make that commitment, imagine that you find yourself sitting back in the nature scene, but all the different elements from each quarter have dissolved, and you feel this deep connection to nature in this beautiful scene.

And now we're going to come out of it by rubbing your hands together, keeping your eyes shut.

And then place your hands over your closed eyes, breathe in and exhale. Then you can rub your hairline… your face… the throat… back of the neck, just coming back into this space… and just allow yourself to arrive.

Now write down all the answers that came to you during this visualization. You have your pact.

And…ACTION!

You're leaving this book with a plan.

You know what you're here to influence.

You know who you're meant to be.

If you know how to start, start now.

If you're not sure how to start, align yourself with someone already working on this change, and work with them.

And may you come to know yourself as a blessing to this world—a blessing the world will feel long after you leave it.

www.ingramcontent.com/pod-product-compliance
Lightning Source LLC
Chambersburg PA
CBHW030005050426
42451CB00006B/119